Capybara

A Complete Owner's Guide

Facts & Information: Habitat, Diet, Health, Breeding, Care, and much more all covered.

Foreword

Until I began volunteering at my local zoo, I had never even heard of a capybara. Since the staff wasn't going to turn me loose cleaning out the tiger cages, I was assigned to be a docent in the petting zoo. The most dangerous animal in that group was a rather elderly billy goat with an attitude.

My chores were benign and actually rather meditative. Here I was, living in a large city, and being handed a rake three days a week with instructions to "clean up the barnyard."

This rarely involved much more than shooing some chickens out of the way, stopping to coo over the rabbits, and occasionally making more mud for the piglets. I was in heaven!

Animals and playing in the dirt? What more can a grown-up kid ask for?

Then one day the petting zoo director informed us that we would be getting two new residents, a pair of female capybaras that were still juveniles.

The first time I saw the strange animals with their blunt, squared off snouts "in person," I had no real basis of comparison for their odd looks.

There was something mildly beaver-like about the capybaras, and I was assured that they were indeed rodents, the largest of their kind in the world, and distant relatives of the beaver.

Since that time I've seen them likened to enormous guinea pigs or even the world's biggest hamsters, but those descriptions aren't quite right to my eye. For one thing, capybaras have oddly delicate feet. At times they almost "prance," and they can move like the very wind.

The capybaras came to us without names, and since all the docents were "women of a certain age," the new additions were promptly dubbed Eleanor Rigby and Michelle.

I honestly don't know what I expected of the capybaras, but they were a wonderful surprise, bright and intelligent, affectionate, and amazingly gentle.

Over the coming year, as they grew bigger and bigger, the capybaras actually became even sweeter, interacting lovingly with the children and rapidly becoming crowd favorites.

Several parents asked during that year if a capybara could be a pet. At first I consistently replied in the negative, but then I learned that the capybara has found its way into the exotic pet trade. Since they do have superior personalities, I'm not all that surprised.

As is the case with many exotics, however, a capybara is not just an animal you run out and adopt on a whim. When they are small, they can be kept in the house, but they don't stay small.

There is also the problem of their highly social nature. Unless you can devote all of your time to being with your pet, a capybara should never be housed alone. They are herd animals with complex emotions and can suffer from terrible separation anxiety.

From my own experience, I would never discourage anyone from keeping a capybara per se, but I do want to say from the beginning that you have to be able to create the right environment – for the animals' sake and for your own.

The following text is a compilation of my research into keeping pet capybaras. Yes, I admit, I was tempted. Every time I go to the zoo, Eleanor and Michelle run to greet me. They clearly remember me and are glad to see me.

I thought I had enough "experience" to possibly have a pair of capybaras, but the more I learned, I realized what a disservice it would be to the animals if I were to try to keep them in my backyard as I had originally planned.

Not only do I not have enough room to keep the animals securely, I live in a neighborhood controlled by a homeowners association. Nothing about the situation was going to work for the capybaras or the neighbors.

Since my decision making process was rather long and involved, and was complicated by the remarkably small number of domestic sources for acquiring a capybara, I have decided to compile my research into this guide.

Whether you decide you can keep a capybara or not, I think you will come away with a different perception of what some folks who are not in the "know" insist on calling the world's largest rat.

With no insult intended to rats, capybaras are more like super intelligent dogs by nature. I have to content myself with frequent visits to my zoo dwelling friends, but there is still a part of me that would love to be able to have capybaras of my own.

Unlike many exotic species present in the pet trade, capybaras are not threatened in the wild. Therefore, it is not inherently unethical to keep them as pets.

The question I always ask potential adopters of any species is, "Can you give this animal the kind of home and care it needs and deserves?"

I had to honestly answer no. I hope by the end of this text, you can give an honest answer of your own. Do right by the animal, and in the end, you'll always do right by yourself and make the correct choice.

Acknowledgments

I would like to express my gratitude towards my family, friends, and colleagues for their kind co-operation and encouragement which helped me in completion of this book.

I would like to express my special gratitude and thanks to my loving husband for his patience, understanding, and support.

My thanks and appreciations also go to my colleagues and people who have willingly helped me out with their abilities.

Additional thanks to my children, whose love and care for our family pets inspired me to write this book.

Table of Contents

Table of Contents

Table of Contents

Table of Contents

Table of Contents

Chapter 1 - Understanding the Capybara

When you first look at a capybara, you won't quite understand what kind of animal you're seeing. They appear to be a cross between an overgrown guinea pig and a beaver, which is appropriate, since they are related to both animals.

The capybara is native to almost all regions of South America except Chile, and is the world's largest rodent. They are also kin to the porcupine, mara, and more distantly to the chinchilla and agouti.

In their native habitat, the capybara is called a "water hog." The species is not threatened, and enjoys population stability in part because they breed easily and prolifically.

Threats

Capybara are hunted for their pelts and meat. A grease derived from their skin is used in pharmaceuticals, and the hide itself makes an unusually high-quality leather.

Farmers mistakenly view the animals as competitors for prime grazing land with domesticated livestock, primarily cattle, and kill them as nuisance pests.

These pressures have not, however, affected the wide distribution of the species, and capybaras actually benefit from deforestation that creates more available grassland.

Populations of capybara living along rivers do disappear in the presence of intense human populations, but overall, the species has proven remarkably adaptable and enduring.

Native Habitat

Capybara are semi-aquatic, and prefer areas of dense forest near rivers, lakes, swamps, marshes, or ponds as well as flooded savannas.

One of their favorite pastimes is wallowing in mud, which they do when the heat rises at midday. In the afternoon and early evening they graze, then rest until midnight before continuing to feed until dawn.

Agile and swift, they can reach speeds over short distances comparable to that of a horse and seemingly turn on a dime. Capybaras are also superb swimmers and can remain submerged for as long as five minutes.

Physical Characteristics

A capybara vaguely resembles a barrel with legs. They are heavy animals with brownish to red fur covering the upper body, yellowish hair on their bellies, and vestigial tails.

There are no color or coat variations. The hair is wiry in texture and sheds only a few coarse strands at a time. As adults, their hair is thinly dispersed, which can make them easily subject to sunburn. They have no odor.

Size and Weight

Adults reach a maximum length of 3.51-4.40 feet (107-134 cm) and are 20-25 inches (50-64 cm) tall at the withers, the highest part of the back near the neck.

Their average weight is 77-146 lbs. (35-66 kg), with some wild specimens topping out at 162 lbs. (73.5 kg). Females tend to be somewhat heavier than males.

In stature, the hind legs are a little higher than the front. There are four toes on the front feet and three on the back, all slightly webbed.

Head and Jaws

The heavy heads end in blunt muzzles with small eyes and ears located near the top of the head. Since they lack a perpendicular jaw hinge, they chew their food in a grinding side-to-side motion.

They are somewhat similar to cattle in that they will often regurgitate their food to chew it again. Capybaras are also coprophagous, eating their own feces to maintain their gut flora and to more efficiently digest the high cellulose content of their diet.

Like most rodents, capybara's teeth grow continually to compensate for the wearing action of their diet. They are born with a complete set of teeth and are ready to eat "adult" food immediately.

Also, like guinea pigs, they cannot synthesize Vitamin C and require supplementation to avoid issues with scurvy, a common health problem in this species.

To have healthy bones, capybaras require adequate amounts of sunlight, and will suffer debilitating deterioration if kept indoors constantly or in a shed with no sunny yard.

Scent Marking

Capybaras have one scent gland on the snout called a morillo and an anal gland also used for scent marking. These structures are present in both genders, but are larger and more prominent in males.

The dark, hairless morillo is clearly visible as a raised semi-oval lump on the snout of males. It secretes copious amounts of a sticky, white fluid. The anal glands in males are lined with detachable hairs coated in a crystalline secretion. Both substances adhere to objects as a mark of territoriality.

Scent marking is accomplished either by rubbing an object with the morillo, walking over something to disperse the anal hairs, or by urinating.

Females typically do not mark territory with urine, and on a whole mark less frequently than males unless they are in estrus.

Vocalizations

Capybaras communicate with a host of vocalizations that range from a very dog-like bark to an "eep" that is similar to a "wheek" in a guinea pig. They also growl, whistle, and whinny. As infants, capybaras let out an almost constant guttural purr.

They are highly communicative with one another and with the humans with whom they bond. Owner blogs are full of stories of their capybaras waking them up for breakfast, and communicating reactions spanning the spectrum from excitement and curiosity to annoyance.

Capybaras seem to possess an uncanny amount of emotional intelligence and pick up easily on their owner's moods. For this reason they respond well to verbal praise and by nature are anxious to please.

Listen to the sounds your pets make and try to imitate the vocalizations when appropriate. Capybaras seem to especially enjoy this kind of "talk," and will carry on complete conversations with you, even if you have absolutely no idea what you're saying!

They also really like it when you get own on their level and act like one of the "herd."

Life Span

In captivity, a capybara lives 8-12 years. In the wild, however, they easily fall prey to jaguars, pumas, eagles, caimans, and the anaconda among other predators. Consequently, the average age at death is four years.

Capybaras submerge themselves in water for minutes at a time to escape predators and will even sleep in the water with only their noses exposed. As needed they can close both their noses and ears to protect these orifices from an influx of water.

Social Behavior

Capybara groups graze on home ranges of about 25 acres (10 hectares) eating both grass and aquatic vegetation. They will eat fruit if it is available, and tree bark, but they are highly selective.

They are extremely gregarious and social animals and typically live in groups of 10-20. These units consist of 2-4 adult males, 4-7 adult females, and a number of juveniles.

The social structure is a hierarchy built around a dominant male. Subordinate males serve distinct roles on the periphery of the group, playing lookout at night and signaling the herd with alarm calls in the event of danger.

Do They Make Good Pets?

Like many exotic animals with unusually good natures, the capybara has been brought into the pet trade. Just because they are kept as companion animals, however, does not necessarily mean this is a good idea.

Before you consider adopting a capybara as a pet, you should carefully consider each of the following factors.

Highly Specific Habitat Needs

Because capybaras are semi-aquatic, they must have access to both water and mud. They prefer to defecate in water, and they use mud to cool down and to protect themselves from potential sunburn.

Although they can be taught to defecate in dry pans, they still must have enough water to submerge, and preferably to swim, which means owners should have some amount of outside space for their pets.

Social Herd Animals

Domestication involves more than an animal simply living in harmony with man. The animal's needs must be met in both a physical and emotional sense for the arrangement to be successful and mutually beneficial.

Capybaras are not just social, they are *intensely* social. They are as intelligent as dogs and crave constant companionship.

If capybaras are kept in a one-on-one relationship with a human, their separation anxiety will go off the charts if left alone. This is true even if you attempt to get the capybara to sleep alone at night.

These animals are most successfully kept in captivity in small groups outdoors. Capybaras are perfectly amenable to human interaction under these circumstances and are highly affectionate, which is why they have become popular in petting zoos.

Learn Well and Are Trainable

Due to their high level of intelligence, a capybara can learn almost anything from a patient owner with an understanding of how to train an animal. These creatures certainly can assimilate what is and is not acceptable behavior.

If they do not receive gentle correction and consistent discipline, a capybara with "inside" privileges will chew the carpet, gnaw the table legs, yank down the curtains, and come up with a whole host of equally creative and destructive "projects."

They are remarkably anxious to please, however, so discipline really need be little more than obvious verbal disapproval.

If this is countered with loving praise for things done well or correctly, a capybara can acquire good "manners" rather quickly. This does not change the fact, however, that they do ultimately grow too large to be exclusively indoor pets.

Try to think of all communication with a capybara as a two-way street. They have a complex communication system within their groups built on vocalizations and body language.

When you become part of their "group" in captivity, a capybara will give as much information as they receive, asking for things they want or enjoy.

In teaching a capybara to do anything, consistent, patient repetition is best. They will respond to whistles, verbal directives, and treats.

They easily learn their names, and will perform various dog-like actions to get food including "twirling," and standing on their hind legs.

House Training

There are many owner stories online about house training capybaras complete with photographs. There's more than enough evidence of success in this arena to silence even the worst naysayer.

When you show one of these animals what to do, and are consistent with your instruction, they are typically quite happy to accommodate you.

It also does not hurt that they are, by nature, very clean and prefer not to soil their habitat, which is excellent if they're living in the house with you!

Having a housebroken capybara works best, however, only when the animal is still small enough to practically live inside. As your capybara grows, it really does need to take its "business" outside.

Since some capybaras will only defecate in water, the growing scope of the potential problems should be readily apparent.

Owners can opt to offer their pets both wet and dry litter trays, but if the capybara wants to be in the water, you automatically have problems.

You're talking about an animal that will weigh 77-146 lbs. (35-66 kg). A "pan" of water may actually be more like a "tub," which means splashing, potential water damage to your home, and difficult clean-up and maintenance for the owner.

Again, just because the capybara can be taught to do something does not mean the doing of it is actually practical in the greater scheme of husbandry.

Ultimately, if you have a capybara, you will have to have outside space to keep the animal. This is not an apartment pet!

Biting and Aggression

Capybaras can bite. In fact, biting is their primary defense. They should not be grabbed quickly, an action they interpret as threatening.

When your capybara has learned to trust you, you can approach the animal more directly. In the beginning, however, it's best to let a capybara initiate most exchanges, especially those that are affectionate, which can make them problematic with overly enthusiastic children.

Capybaras do have distinct personalities. Some individuals will thus be more or less prone to this type of defensive or startled biting behavior. Overall, however, capybaras are gentle and not easily provoked.

Digging and Escapes

Capybaras don't dig, which is a plus in terms of preserving your yard, but as large as they are, these animals will squeeze through the slightest possible crack. They can also push through any kind of flexible wire fencing, so wood fencing is preferable.

Two capybaras can live well in a spacious backyard, but they must have plenty of room to run and play, places to hide, and completely secure fencing.

They must have access to water, so a pond is ideal. Depending on the climate, a shed lined with straw and potentially outfitted with a source of heat will also be necessary.

Under such circumstances, a capybara won't actively seek a means of escape, but if one presents itself, the animals will take advantage of it. A fleet footed and potentially frightened capybara on the loose can be all but impossible to re-capture.

Male or Female?

The question of gender is a standard one in adoption considerations for almost any species. This is not a relevant issue with capybaras, however.

The personalities of both genders are equally good, and the final choice of a companion should be predicated much more on individual personality.

Most pets develop mature natures that are more or less in concert with the kind of attention and husbandry they receive from their owners. A well-cared for capybara is typically a well-behaved capybara.

Capybaras and Other Pets?

Until your capybara reaches a sufficient size to defend itself, all interactions with other animals should be closely supervised. In all likelihood when you acquire your pet it will be about the size of a guinea pig or a large rabbit.

At a young age, either a dog or cat can seriously injure a capybara. The larger the animal grows, the less likely cats are to be interested, but aggressive dogs should be watched at all times.

Although less so than other rodents due to their size, it is still possible for other pets, especially dogs, to see a capybara as prey.

Typically, however, capybaras are gentle giants and get along quite well with other animals. You can get an idea of just how placid they are from the website Animals Sitting on Capybaras at <u>animalssittingoncapybaras.tumblr.com</u>.

Garibaldi Rous, one of the Internet's more famous capybaras that died in February 2014 was well known for his great affection for other animals, including a propensity for hugging cats.

His website, "Capybara Madness: A Pet Capybara's View of the World," at <u>www.gianthamster.com</u>, is an excellent resource for people wanting to explore all facets of life with a pet capybara. The archives span seven years and cover a huge range of topics.

Legal Considerations

As is often the case with the more unusual exotics, laws can be murky regarding capybaras.

In the United States, most states require that prospective owners apply for an import permit from the relevant state agency, generally either the agriculture department or the department of fish, game, and wildlife.

Before the animal can actually be brought into the state, it will be examined by a government veterinarian. This inspection will eliminate the presence of infectious diseases and evaluate the animal's overall health and the quality of the care it has and is receiving.

In addition to the import permit, the owner will typically need to hold and maintain a general license to keep an exotic pet.

This ensures that the individual is accountable for the safe transport and maintenance of the animal, including keeping it in a proper habitat.

Similar laws apply to capybara ownership in the UK. Potential owners must acquire a license to keep the capybara, and should contact their local council for more information.

Applicants should be prepared for their homes to be inspected, and they must present a detailed care plan on which their suitability to own a capybara will be judged.

Estimated Purchase Price

Putting an accurate estimated cost on an animal like a capybara is extremely difficult. If you can find an exotic animal breeder and purchase a captive bred capybara, you will pay around $600 / £360.

If you have to purchase and import a capybara from South America, the price may not be substantially different for the animal itself, but shipping and associated expenses can range from $3,000-$8,000 / £1,804-£4,811.

Pros and Cons of Capybara Ownership

Since these factors could be considered positive or negative based on your own individual perception, I simply want to reiterate some major points in this list.

- Capybaras are large. Individuals average 77-146 lbs. (35-66 kg).

- They do shed, but only a few single hairs at a time. The hairs are wiry and very easy to vacuum up.

- Capybaras have no odor.

- While they are agreeable to interaction, it's best to let them initiate the contact.

- They do not like to be grabbed, and can sometimes be frightened by an unexpected hug.

- They are not aggressive by nature, but they can bite if they are frightened or feel threatened.

- They need access to water in which they can submerge themselves and to mud.

- If they do not have access to mud, they can sunburn.

- They prefer to defecate in water, but will generally be agreeable to using a dry pan.

- They are herd animals and should at least be kept in pairs.

- They do best when kept outside with adequate access to sunlight to maintain the health of their bones.

- They cannot synthesize Vitamin C and are thus susceptible to developing scurvy.

- They are expensive pets, costing at minimum $600, while travel expenses for importation can cost thousands of dollars.

Chapter 2 – Buying a Capybara

Buying a capybara is not an easy process. There are very few breeders with published information online. One of the best sources is ExoticAnimalsForSale.net.

The site allows for searches by animal name, and will return a number of listings at any given time for capybaras, but there are few organized breeding programs represented.

While I was researching this text, I was able to find two USDA certified facilities in Texas, Kapi'yva Exotics (www.kapiyvaexotics.com) and Tri-Lake Exotics (www.trilakesexotics.com).

A third breeder in Arkansas is now retired, but a note on the website indicates she can refer interested parties to other capybara breeders. Her information is:

Mary Lee Stropes
Shad EE Shack Farm
Booneville, Arkansas 72927
www.shadeeshack.com

I was not able to locate any capybara breeders in Europe, although the animals are now found around the world. In July 2013 a runaway from an animal shelter in England was spotted trotting along the bank of the River Thames at the Henley Regatta. The animal remained on the loose for a month before it was recaptured.

Please note that all web addresses and contact information were accurate at the time of this writing, but like all things online, I cannot guarantee how long this material will be valid.

Kapi'yva Exotics

Kapi'yva Exotics at www.kapiyvaexotics.com is a privately run zoological facility near Houston, TX specializing in "the propagation of rare and endangered species and supply[ing] animals to zoos, educators and other licensed entities."

They are accredited by the Zoological Association of America (ZAA), and hold a Texas Parks and Wildlife Department zoological permit and a United States Department of Agriculture class A breeder's license.

The founder of the operation, Justin Dildy, is a member of the Zoological Association of America and the Feline Conservation Federation. Kapi'yva preference is for interested parties to send inquiries via email at kapiyvaexotics@gmail.com.

Tri-Lakes Exotics

Tri-Lake Exotics is also a USDA certified breeder. They are located in Northeast Texas on Farm Road 21 between Mount Pleasant and Mount Vernon. The animals are bottled raised, and socialized daily as well as receiving 24-hour care from an in-house veterinarian.

Contact: Dr. Cathy Cranmore
Email: cathy@trilakesexotics.com
Phone: 903-588-2727

Considering Shipping

The published shipping policy at Kapi'yva states that "local pickup is preferred" and indicates they "may be willing to deliver or meet you half way depending on your location."

They do ship from both Hobby and Intercontinental Airports in Houston, TX but specify that the flights must be arranged through the Delta Pet First fare program or via United Airline's "Pet Safe."

Tri-Lake's shipping policy does not specifically mention capybaras, but indicates the same preference for personal pickup. The policy only discusses airline shipping for

Wallaroo and Kangaroos, but offers the potential of a $3 per mile delivery fee.

Travel Nightmares

In a January 2014 post for the blog "Dobbye the Capybara" www.petcapybara.com/ a capybara owner discusses the true costs, financial and otherwise of acquiring his pet.

"How Much Is That Capybara in the Window?" is a sobering description of just how difficult it can be to both acquire and to move an exotic animal.

The author writes, "Most airlines will not allow rodents in the cabin, so even though your three week old capybara is the size of a guinea pig, it is required to travel in the hold of the plane, down there with the big dogs."

That statement alone makes hardcore animal lovers cringe, but the flight was in cold weather and the poor animal sat with the other "baggage" for an extended period of time until his owner could retrieve him.

Two weeks later, the little capybara almost died of pneumonia. The author observes that if he had it all to do over again, he'd fly out to pick up the capybara, rent a car, and drive home. "At that age, they are tiny, quiet, and manageable, and no motel would ever guess you had a pet with you."

I am personally not a fan of shipping animals. It may be inescapable with a capybara due to their scarcity, and this is an aspect of the "risk factor" of buying one of these animals that you have to consider.

When you contract to purchase a live animal and have it sent to you, the chances of a tragedy occurring in transit are fairly high. Can you live with the guilt if something happens?

Identifying a Healthy Capybara

When you are adopting an unusual animal like a capybara, you need to find out as much as you possibly can about the facility where the animal was born and is being raised in order to judge the condition in which you are likely to receive your new pet.

You want to consider factors like:

Population density and socialization.

Has the capybara had plenty of interaction with other capybaras and with humans? Is this a level of socialization that will make it more or less dependent on you?

For instance, if you are buying a capybara that has lived as a single pet dependent on one caregiver, can you give the same level of care?

If you are buying an animal that is used to being part of a group, can you provide that degree of sociability, preferably with other capybaras?

Remember, you are responsible for the animal's physical and emotional wellbeing. With this species, the emotional component is unusually strong.

Spaciousness and appropriateness of the habitat.

Has the animal had lots of room to play and explore with free access to sources of clean water for both consumption and as an environmental feature?

Smaller animals can be housed successfully indoors and will often be comfortable using a pan to do their "business," but since they will grow too large to be inside exclusively, they should be used to time outside.

Over and above those considerations, capybaras must get adequate time in the sun to be healthy.

Overall condition of the facility.

Is the operation clean and well run? What, if any, certifications does it carry? Are the animals regularly attended by a veterinarian?

Typically breeders are quite happy to show you around their operation and to discuss their animals with you. If a breeder is reluctant to do so, this could be a red flag that something may not be quite right.

Physically Inspecting the Animal

Due to the distance likely involved in your acquisition, you may not be able to physically examine the capybara in advance of your visit to actually retrieve your pet.

Certainly you should have seen photographs, and potentially even observed the capybara on video before moving forward with a deal.

Once on site or when you take possession of the animal, check for potential physical problems and immediately arrange for the capybara to be evaluated by a qualified exotic animal veterinarian.

Eyes

Look closely at the eyes. They should be bright and clear. Some discharge is normal, since capybaras are sensitive to dust and allergens, but there should be no excessive or discolored fluid or mucus.

Ears

Gently look inside the ear. If there is a yeasty, foul smell with visible debris and wax, ear mites may be present. These parasites are a common nuisance in many animal species.

Ear mites are easily treatable, but should not be ignored as they create itching and discomfort for the animal.

You'll need to obtain a topical medication from your veterinarian to eliminate the infestation and the debris in the ear may need to be cleaned out.

Nose

There should be only minimal discharge from the nose, again as a reaction to dust and allergens only, and it should not be discolored or excessive, which could indicate the presence of a respiratory infection.

Mouth

Ask the breeder to help you examine the capybara's teeth. They should be straight and well aligned with no sign of breakage or overgrowth that might prevent the animal from eating properly.

A single broken tooth is typically not a problem, although it may need to be clipped and evened out by a veterinarian. Excessive broken teeth may indicate scurvy, which is caused by Vitamin C deficiency.

Breathing

Listen to the capybara's breathing, which should be quiet, with no clicking sounds indicated respiratory infection. The presence of nasal discharge and irregular breathing is a serious warning sign that should not be ignored.

Overall Condition

The capybara should be in good physical condition in a general sense. It should have no visible swellings or lumps, and any scratches or wounds should be tiny and clearly the result of rough housing.

At a young age, a capybara should not show signs of dominance fighting that may include bites and more serious wounds.

If such wounds are present on an older animal, find out what happened. Try to determine if the capybara in question has exhibited a tendency to be aggressive.

Demeanor

Young capybaras are quiet and easily managed, but should still be bright, curious, and energetic when at play, especially with others of their own kind.

Capybaras prefer to be the instigators of affection, but you should see signs of regular interaction when the capybara responds to the breeder or other animals in the vicinity.

Estimated Costs

As I mentioned in Chapter 1, the price of a capybara itself is roughly on par with that of a large pedigreed dog, typically around $600 / £360.

The ancillary costs of shipping the animal, however, could easily climb into thousands of dollars, and then there is the matter of constructing an appropriate habitat including water features.

In my opinion, it is absolutely impossible to arrive at an accurate estimate of costs since every situation will be completely unique.

I will say, however, that capybaras are not inexpensive pets. If you cannot afford the cost of creating the kind of environment these animals require, seriously reconsider the idea of acquiring one.

Chapter 3 – Daily Care of a Capybara

Make no mistake; people who decide to keep capybaras as pets are willing to make a lot of modifications to their homes and lives to accommodate these giant rodents.

If you search online you'll find stories from capybara owners who have installed extra toilets into which they dump the approximately one gallon / 3.78 liters of feces their pet produces each day.

You'll read about dedicated owners who haven't been on a vacation in years because their pets don't like to be left and won't tolerate being cared for by a stranger.

But rather than talking about these and other experiences with frustration, the tone is more one of resigned affection. Clearly people who have capybaras as pets love them and do these and other things quite willingly to create a good atmosphere for their beloved animal companions.

Capybaras are not necessarily complicated pets to keep on a daily basis, but they aren't low maintenance. If you have only one, you must be prepared to be your pet's constant companion.

The following discussion assumes, for the most part, that you will be keeping at least a pair of capybaras in an outside setting.

Like all animals, capybaras will benefit in every possible way from good husbandry practices. When they receive high quality nutrition and are kept in spacious, clean habitats, they are hardy animals with few health problems.

This provision for health does not just extend to physical issues, however, it also includes their psychological wellbeing, which is predicated on an understanding of their innate herd mentality.

Keeping Captive Groups

Due to their highly social nature, it's best to keep capybaras in a group of two or three. An optimum mix is one male and two females.

If males are housed together there will be fighting, but even females will display aggression if kept in an overly small habitat.

The bottom line is simple. Capybaras need room and they need company.

Avoiding Unplanned Litters

Obviously if you are keeping a mixed group of capybaras you will need to take measures to avoid unplanned litters of pups. The easiest way to do this is to have the male neutered. The surgery should be performed when the animal is 6-9 months of age.

It is extremely important that you find an exotic animal veterinarian to perform the procedure, preferably one who has previous experience with capybaras or one who can confer with more specialized vets about the surgery.

If performed incorrectly, bruising around the testicles can affect the function of the animal's hind legs. Also, capybaras are very sensitive to drugs, a topic that will be discussed fully in the chapter on health.

Room for Just One?

If you cannot keep a group of capybaras, think carefully before proceeding. A lone capybara is going to demand a tremendous amount of your time and attention.

Again, these are SOCIAL animals. They live in groups in nature. They do not like to be alone and if they bond to you exclusively, they won't just want your company, they will actually need it.

This fact can complicate things if you decide later on to create a capybara group by acquiring a "friend" for you existing pet. The original capybara may not react well to someone trying to interact with "his" human.

Introducing New Group Members

Adult capybaras bond closely to one another and to their keepers, making the introduction of new group members more complicated. If not handled slowly and carefully, established adults will attack and kill newcomers.

There is no exact science to the introductions, but a good method is to allow the animals to see and smell one another through a safe barrier like a temporary wire fence.

Never just turn a new capybara in with an established group. Even after a segregated period of acclimatization, be prepared to supervise and potentially separate the animals should aggression become an issue.

Habitat and Shelter

With any species of animal kept as a companion animal, the same rule of thumb applies to habitat design or enclosure selection. Construct or buy the largest space you can afford and accommodate.

At minimum, two to three capybaras can be kept in an outside enclosure that is 12 feet x 20 feet / 3.65 meters x 6.09 meters for a total 240 square feet / 22.3 square meters.

A large doghouse will serve as a proper shelter for capybaras unless you are in an extreme climate where a heated shelter will be necessary in the winter.

Make sure the enclosure is at least 3 feet x 5 feet / 0.914 meters x 1.524 meters for a total of 15 square feet / 1.393 square meters.

Fencing

To prevent escapes by jumping, incorporate a fence or similar barrier that is at least 6 feet / 1.8 meters high. Capybaras can get over anything shorter, but they do not dig, so there is no need to construct any special footing on the barrier. Since they will exploit gaps in fencing and can take down flexible wire net, solid wood panels are generally best.

Beyond these considerations for containment, you can create virtually any kind of habitat. Because capybara ownership is still unusual, it's a good idea to explore the relevant websites included in the back of the book to look for creative husbandry ideas.

Some of the sites are for blogs "kept" by pet capybaras. These "first person" accounts are highly insightful in terms of habitat design, daily care regimens, and ongoing interaction with these unique animals.

What works for one person and one capybara may not work for another, but all of these sites are excellent sources of information.

A Pool or Tank

Your capybaras' habitat should include an area for sun and shade with at least one (and preferably more) sources of water. Remember that your pets are semi-aquatic. When they are frightened, their natural impulse is to hide in the water.

Provide pools with sloping bottoms that begin at a depth of 3.5 feet. / 1.07 meters and gradually increase to 6 feet / 1.84 meters.

Your pets should be able to submerge completely if they desire to do so. Remember that water not only serves as a place of refuge for capybaras, but also allows the animals to cool off during the heat of the day.

Also, many capybaras prefer to defecate and urinate in the water. This means that pond / water tank cleaning is a very large part of capybara husbandry, and one you should figure into your habitat design ideas.

Room to Swim

In the best of all possible scenarios, capybaras won't just have a pool in which they can submerge, but one in which they can actually swim. In the water, these animals are incredibly graceful and agile.

They love to perform aquatic acrobatics with absolute abandon, diving and rolling with an enviable freedom. This leads many owners to assume that giving their pets access to a human swimming pool is the perfect solution. This is actually not the case at all.

Chlorine and chemicals used in pool water to kill harmful bacteria create a potential hazard to your capybaras that is made more serious by the compounding effect of evaporation. This leads to an even greater concentration of chemicals over time.

Because capybaras drink the water in which they swim, allowing your pets to use a human swimming pool exposes them to toxins that may kill the beneficial bacteria in the animals' guts that are essential for proper digestion.

If possible, it's better to give your capybaras their own pool, which is cleaned regularly to control the growth of algae and to prevent fouling from a buildup of feces.

While this is not practical for all capybara owners, access to deep water for swimming is a superb augmentation of your pets' habitat.

Temperature and Humidity

Capybaras are well equipped to withstand fairly substantial temperature variations. With a heated shelter and adequate bedding, they can tolerate outdoor temperatures of 10 F / - 12 C on one extreme, and as much as 90-100 F / 32-38 C on the other if they have water and shade.

Obviously this is attractive from a husbandry standpoint as it increases the range of climates in which a capybara is a viable companion animal.

They are equally adaptable to varying humidity levels and appear to be unaffected by readings in a range of anywhere from 15% to 70%.

Lighting

It is obviously most beneficial for this species to be housed in groups outdoors, however, if they are kept indoors for any extended period of time, including inclement weather, strive for a 12-hour light/dark cycle. Either incandescent or fluorescent lighting works equally well.

Substrate and Bedding

In a naturally planted outdoor enclosure, soil and grass work fine as a substrate. The floor of the animals' enclosed shelter can be concrete, which makes clean-up much easier.

Since capybaras like mud, hosing down portions of the habitat not only helps you clean, but provides an even more natural and stimulating setting.

Hay makes excellent bedding for the animals and is also edible. Use clean hay that smells fresh and is free of dust and debris like thorns, twigs, and burrs.

Accessories

Capybaras do not require any kind of "furniture" for climbing or sitting, but plants that create visual barriers and hiding spots are necessary.

Logs serve the same purpose, as well as providing additional material for chewing and gnawing. Add rocks to increase the natural elements of the setting, and incorporate hay bales to wall off areas that will create a sense of security and seclusion for your pets.

Habitat Maintenance

Clean the capybaras' habitat daily, removing wet and soiled bedding, accumulated feces, and any uneaten food. Again, you will be dealing, on average, with about a gallon / 3.78 liters of feces each day. Plan on how you will dispose of that material.

Since the animals will also defecate in the water, their pools or tanks should be drained, cleaned, and disinfected on a weekly basis if not more often. This means you will need to be able to handle the volume of wastewater as well as the fecal material.

Additionally, capybaras scent mark items in their enclosure that may become saturated and require periodic replacement.

Inside Time

Even if your capybara lives outside, there will be times when you want to bring your pet in the house. In order to do this safely, you must only let the animal in areas that have been prepared in advance for the presence of a very large rodent.

Like house rabbits, capybaras will bite on cords and chew exposed wires, but remember that their size will also allow them to topple over the appliances attached to those cords! Unless you want your big screen TV crashing down in the wake of a capybara pulling on the wires, don't let your pet in that part of your house!

Until your pet is large enough to barge right through them, use baby gates to section off acceptable areas and stay with your capybara at all times when it's inside.

Digestion and Nutrition

Capybaras have a digestive system that is quite similar to that of a rabbit and like rabbits, they are herbivores. They have a simple stomach, but also a large pouch in their intestine called a cecum.

The cecum produces a special form of paste-like feces, which the animal re-ingests. This allows them to maximize their nutrients and to better digest the high cellulose content of their primarily grass-based diet.

Capybaras also regurgitate and re-chew their food while resting after the fashion of cows chewing their cud.

In the wild, they graze selectively, taking in about 6.5 lbs. / 3 kg of plant material per day. Depending on availability, aquatic plants can make up as little as .6% of their diet and as much as 87%.

Wild capybaras will go into fields to eat grain, squash, melons, sweet potatoes, bananas, corn, and manioc leaves. These natural tastes allow them to be fed easily in captivity.

Feeding

Put your capybaras on a twice per day feeding routine. Since their diet in the wild is primarily short grasses, hay is a major staple of their nutrition. In addition, any of the following are acceptable:

commercial rodent chow
monkey chow
kale
endive
spinach
romaine
yams
corn
apples
bananas
carrots
broccoli
pears
apples
potatoes
raw peanuts
cantaloupe
watermelon
bamboo foliage

Make sure that no food be allowed to mold or to become contaminated with feces in the enclosure. Remove all uneaten food on a daily basis.

Please note that rhododendrons, azaleas, and pieris are all extremely toxic to capybaras. Make sure your pets do not come into contact with these plants under any circumstances!

Hay as a Staple

Good quality hay is a staple of capybara health, providing your pet not only with a source of nutrition, but also a means of wearing down its teeth. The grinding action of chewing the hay prevents overgrowth and the formation of dental spurs.

Good hay smells clean and dry with no suggestion of mold or dust. High fiber hays that offer a good protein mix are ideal. Some combination of the following will work well:

- timothy
- mountain grass
- brome
- orchard grass
- alfalfa

Of this, alfalfa is the richest. If you are just introducing alfalfa into your pet's diet, do so slowly to avoid gastrointestinal upset. The same is true of clover hay, which should be used sparingly.

Timothy hay is considered a "standard" and is affordable, selling in packages of 5-50 lbs. / 2.26-22.7 kg in a price range of $20-$65 / £12-£40.

(Depending on the number of capybaras you are keeping, you may want to investigate a local source for hay and buy it by the bale.)

Food Containers

Although you can opt to dispense hay from a rack, the capybaras will scatter it no matter what. In order to avoid mealtime aggression, it's much easier to simply offer all food stuffs in large wooden trays that allow more than one adult to feed at a time.

In order to enhance your pets' level of intellectual stimulation, considering hiding some food items throughout the enclosure. This will encourage natural foraging behaviors and get your pets to exercise more.

Hydration

Capybaras must have fresh drinking water at all times, but since they will defecate in their bowls or troughs, multiple water bottles with ball bearing "lixit" tips are an especially good option. They prevent fouling of the water and are much more easily cleaned.

Harness and Leash

Capybaras take quite well to being outfitted with a harness and walking on a leash. This affords owners a good way of controlling their pets for grazing excursions and walks.

Since you'll be hard pressed to find a harness especially for a capybara, look at dog harnesses for animals weighing around 100 lbs. / 45.35 kg or more.

You want the harness to fit snuggly, with just enough room for you to insert a couple of fingers under the straps. Unfortunately, due to their barrel-like build, harnesses do tend to slide right off capybaras, especially if they get one foot through a strap.

Many owners solve this problem by making their pets wear two harnesses, so if one fails, they still have control of the animal. You will likely have to experiment to find what works best with your pet.

The major goal is to make sure the capybara is safely contained and that you are in control of the situation. A leash of any length will work. Retractable leashes are a good option since they can be adjusted to so many lengths.

Chapter 4 – Health Care for Your Capybara

With good husbandry practices, well-rounded nutrition, and an adequate amount of sunlight, capybaras in captivity are hearty animals. They don't require vaccinations, and they don't need any specialized medical care, but could benefit from being wormed annually.

They have extremely strong immune systems and are naturally resistant to bacteria. Capybaras are highly susceptible to runny eyes and noses, however, but only because they are sensitive to dust and allergens. These problems are rarely a cause for serious concern.

Truthfully, the most common health problem with which owners are confronted is small wounds from dominance confrontations. Exposure to toxins in the environment is also a concern.

Cuts and Scrapes

In additional to territorial scuffles, capybaras can also be a little clumsy, and they play rough. Small cuts and scrapes are very common with these pets and should be cleaned at least twice a day and left uncovered to heal.

Such wounds should be treated with betadine, chlorhexidine solution, or any common antiseptic spray. If the cut is deep, access to swimming and mud should be temporarily restricted.

Parasites and Mange Mites

Like all animals that live outside, capybaras can be prone to intestinal parasites. If the animals don't have adequate access to water, they can also be infested with mange mites.

Ivermectin 1% administered orally at a dose of .02 cc per lb of body weight can be used to address these problems, but should not be given more than once a week. The medicine can either be squirted into the mouth or mixed with your pet's food.

Scurvy from Vitamin C Deficiency

Like their close relative the guinea pig, capybaras cannot produce Vitamin C and must get what they need from their diet or from supplementation.

If Vitamin C deficiency or scurvy develops, the animals will experience abnormalities of the blood and bones including bleeding in the muscles, joints, ribs, and intestines. Other symptoms include:

- Overall lethargy and weakness with an unwillingness to move around and interact as normal.

- Changes in movement and gait due to stiffened or enlarged joints.

- A diminished appetite accompanied by weight loss and generally by diarrhea.

- Evident body pain to the point of crying out if touched. There may also be some breaking down of the skin.

You can certainly feed your pet commercial guinea pig chow, which has added Vitamin C, but this solution can be pricey. An easier method is simply to sprinkle ascorbic acid powder on your pet's food several times a week.

It's important that a veterinarian examine the capybara to determine if other problems are present in concert with the scurvy.

Dental Malocclusion

Since capybaras' teeth grow throughout their lives, your pet must receive adequate amounts of hay to keep their incisors and molars worn down.

Capybaras don't play with toys like smaller rodents, but they will chew on tree bark and even branches.

If the animals' teeth are allowed to overgrow, they can development misalignments called malocclusions that will prevent them from eating normally.

Only a vet is qualified to trim the animal's teeth backs safely. This procedure is not something you should try on our own.

The Issue of Environmental Toxins

Beyond the very simple health problems cited here, capybaras are highly sensitive to a host of environmental toxins, like those I've already discussed in relation to allowing the animals to swim in human pools.

The Internet's best known capybara, Garibaldi Rous, whose life is chronicled at www.gianthamster.com, died in January 2014 of chronic liver damage.

Even following a necropsy, the cause of the damage could not be determined, but some potential culprits could include:

- low levels of dietary toxins
- the anesthesia used when the animal was neutered
- pesticides on grass he may have ingested
- a genetic defect

The mystery of his death is a sadly common situation among captive capybaras because good veterinary information about their health is severely limited.

The Problem of Capybara Health Care

After Garibaldi's death, his owner established The ROUS Foundation at gianthamster.com/rousfoundation.

The foundation helps to cover the costs of necropsies on captive capybaras including shipping of the deceased animal to the Texas A&M University College of Veterinary Medicine from within the United States and Canada.

On a case-by-case basis, funding may also be provided for treatment of capybaras with various health conditions. The greater mission of the Foundation is to gather more information about the cause of death in captive capybaras in order to develop better treatment strategies.

For instance, while it is widely known that these animals are sensitive to anesthesia, there is no established anesthesia protocol for the species.

These concerns make finding a good exotic animal veterinarian for your pet capybara both crucial and difficult.

Finding an Exotic Animal Vet

It is extremely unlikely that you will find a veterinarian with experience treating capybaras. It will be helpful, however, if you can find a vet who has treated other kinds of rodents.

Depending on your location, your only resources may be a small animal vet or one who primarily treats livestock. It is imperative that any vet with whom you work understand that captive capybaras are highly sensitive to antibiotics and anesthesia.

Since many other species have these same issues, the vet should already know the safest medications to use with your pet, or have the ability to reach out to specialists at veterinary teaching institutions to get more information.

Most vets who have never seen a capybara will tend to regard the animals as livestock, when it would be more helpful to think of them after the fashion of guinea pigs and rabbits, especially in regard to digestive issues.

Given the time and expense of acquiring a capybara, I highly recommend that you interview vets well in advance of adopting your pet. If you will have no viable access to health care for the capybara in the event of illness, you should reconsider the wisdom of proceeding with the adoption.

Chapter 5 – Breeding Capybaras

Capybaras reproduce via a system of polygynous breeding, meaning there is one dominant male in the group that pairs with several females.

Sexual Maturity and Fertility

Females are sexually mature at 7-12 months of age with males maturing at 15-24 months.

The estrus cycle of the female capybara is quite short, only 7.5 days, and they are receptive to males for only 8 hours.

Although this would seem like a limited window of opportunity, the species still breeds easily and prolifically.

Capybara Mating

In wild groups, the dominant males jealously guard females, frequently sniffing for the proper mating time. For their part, females whistle to attract males.

The pair will mate in the water, with the male entering the water and then swimming back and forth in front of the female until she accepts him.

Copulation is brief, and often takes place with the female submerged. If a female does not want to mate, she will dive deeply enough into the water to dislodge the male attempting to mount her.

It is also not unusual for a mating pair to be interrupted by the arrival of a second opportunistic male.

There is no specific mating season. Capybaras breed year round, but in wild groups, there is a peak at the beginning of the wet season.

Pregnancy and Birth

Under good conditions, females have one to two litters each year. The entire group raises the offspring. Communities of fewer than four adult capybaras in the wild are not successful in raising their young to adulthood.

Females experience a 150-day gestation and give birth to 4-5 pups. The overall breeding group will have as many as 15 pups present at any one time.

Capybara Pups

When they are born, a capybara pup weighs about 3.3 lbs. (1500 grams). They are born with all of their teeth fully erupted, and they can follow their mothers and begin to eat grass shortly after birth.

Pups nurse for approximately 16 weeks, often indiscriminately from several females in the group. Very young capybaras ride on the backs of females and avoid going into the water where they are at great danger from both caiman and anaconda.

Chapter 6 – Frequently Asked Questions

Capybaras are so unusual the very sight of one begins to engender all kinds of questions. Some of the more frequently asked include the following.

How big do they really get?

An adult capybara can reach a maximum length of around 3.51-4.40 feet (107-134 cm). At the highest point of the body, right behind the neck, they stand around 20-25 inches (50-64 cm) tall.

Average captive weights fall in a range of 77-146 lbs. (35-66 kg). By comparison, a really large male Golden Retriever will weigh around 77 lbs. (35 kg.) At the very least, your capybaras will be that size and probably larger.

What are rodents, anyway?

There are more than 1,800 species of rodents in the world, of which the capybara is the largest. All are mammals, and all have the same distinguishing feature, teeth that grow throughout their lives.

Rodents must have something on which to chew to keep their teeth worn down. For smaller pets like mice and rats, wooden chew toys are typically provided. Capybaras need to keep their teeth worn down on a steady diet of hay with tree bark also provided.

Of the larger family of rodents, capybaras are most closely related to guinea pigs, chinchillas, and other cavies.

What is the second largest rodent?

Second place for size in the rodent world goes to the Patagonian cavy or mara. They stand about a foot tall (30.48 cm) and typically weigh 25 lbs. / 11.33 kg. Unlike the semi-aquatic capybara, maras live in dry grasslands. They look somewhat like small deer.

Where do capybaras live in the wild?

Because capybaras are semi-aquatic, they prefer grasslands and forests adjacent to sources of water like lakes, rivers, and streams. They are indigenous to all the countries of South America except Chile.

Particularly high concentrations of capybaras are found in the Pantanal in Brazil and the Llanos in Columbia. Both regions are spacious grasslands that flood annually.

When are capybaras most active?

Capybaras are crepuscular animals, showing their greatest level of activity at dawn and dusk. They rest during the heat of the day, often in water, and will develop sunburns if they don't have access to shade.

As evening comes on, they begin to forage again, then resting until midnight before grazing until dawn. However, in areas where they are heavily hunted, capybaras will become nocturnal.

Do capybaras have special adaptations?

Capybaras have webbed feet that help them both to swim and to negotiate muddy ground. Their surprisingly delicate gait is designed to help them test the softness of the ground ahead before they place their full weight into the step.

The high placement of their eyes, ears, and noses allow them to see and breathe while swimming. They have the ability to block both their ears and noses to keep water from flooding these orifices.

Consequently, they can remain submerged for as long as five minutes, which is their primary means of hiding from predators in the wild.

Is it true that a capybara can get a sunburn?

Fully-grown capybaras have coarse hair spread thinly over their skin. It does not cover their skin sufficiently to protect them against sunburn, which is why they rest in the water or in shade and also wallow in mud.

How do capybaras use pools of water?

A deep pond of water is an essential aspect of capybara husbandry. The animals dive into the water when they are afraid and when they need to cool off. Many prefer to defecate in water, and mating occurs while submerged.

In addition to these life functions, capybaras just plain love water! They are superb swimmers, exhibiting extreme grace, and appear to have a great deal of fun doing it!

What is the raised structure on the nose?

Both male and female capybaras have a scent gland on the nose called a morillo, which is dark and hairless. In males, however, the structure is much more prominent. The animals mark their territory by rubbing objects, other capybaras, and even you!

Do capybaras make noises?

Capybaras make many noises, most difficult to describe. You will hear whistles, clicking, grunts, and purring from young animals.

Capybaras also bark when they need to alert their group of nearby danger. In the wild, this may be a signal for the group to rush into the water and form a protective cluster.

How large are capybara groups?

In the wild, capybaras will live in groups of 10-20 around a single dominant male. They range over about 25-50 acres (10-20 hectares).

Capybara groups will always be relatively close to a source of water, particularly during the dry season. The females participate in co-parenting all the juveniles, with the inferior males serving largely as lookouts at the periphery of the group.

What do capybaras eat?

Wild capybaras live primarily on a diet of grasses and aquatic plants as well as melons and squashes where they are available. Adults consume about 8 lbs. / 3.62 kg of grass daily.

Isn't grass hard to digest?

Yes, grass is hard to digest so capybaras have a special chamber in the intestine that forms pellets called cecotropes, which the animals re-ingest in a practice called coprophagy. This helps the capybara digest the high levels of cellulose in its diet and still get all the nutrients it requires.

What are the capybara's natural predators?

The capybara's natural predators include jaguars, anacondas, and caiman. Infant and juvenile capybaras are highly vulnerable to foxes, vultures, and wild dogs.

Unfortunately, capybaras are also preyed upon by humans. The animals' skin is made into leather, and the meat is consumed as food. The consistency is something like pork, but with a mildly fishy taste.

How long do capybaras live?

In the wild, capybaras live 8-10 years although most die around age 4. In captivity, they can easily live to age 12.

Are capybaras endangered?

Although ranchers kill capybaras out of a fear that they are a competition for domestic grazing animals, this is not actually the case. Capybaras prefer the short vegetation that grows near sources of water, while cattle like taller, drier vegetation.

Although capybaras are hunted extensively for meat and for their hides, which are used to make leather, they are not endangered. In fact, they are found throughout South America in good numbers.

Afterword

Since my own experience helping to care for two capybaras in a petting zoo, I've wished I could keep a pair of these gentle giants. It's difficult to explain to someone that the world's largest rodent is also one of the sweetest animals I've ever encountered.

My research convinced me that trying to keep a couple of capybaras in the backyard would not only be detrimental to the animals' health and wellbeing, but would probably lock me in a losing fight with my homeowners association.

Never mind that capybaras are clean, quiet, have no odor, and do not carry deadly diseases. People hear "big rat," and their tolerance levels drop into the basement.

The real reason I abandoned my plan, however, was that I couldn't give a pair of capybaras the room they needed, nor could I afford to dig a swimming pool specifically for their use.

Now, technically, a pool might not be necessary, but there's no denying that capybaras are happier and healthier when they have adequate access to water in which they can swim and they can't use human swimming pools.

The chemicals used to treat the water are entirely too toxic, and big or not, capybaras are highly susceptible to toxins. Even if you don't go as large as a swimming pool, they still need enough water in which to submerge themselves.

Hopefully after having read this book you will see clearly that capybaras have highly specific husbandry needs that involve their psychological as well as physical health.

They are definitely not a pet for everyone. Ultimately they grow too large to be kept indoors, and they suffer from severe separation anxiety. Capybaras must either be kept in groups, or you have to be home and with your pet pretty much constantly.

Now, the reward for that is 8-12 years with an unusual, highly intelligent, extremely devoted, and affectionate creature. Many people are so smitten with capybaras they want one after just a few minutes of initial interaction.

It's imperative that you exercise good judgment before going forward with a plan to adopt one or more capybaras. I strongly suggest you spend some time on the relevant websites listed in the back of this book. Read as many first-person experiences as possible.

Put the animal's welfare first in your consideration. If you can't give capybaras the kind of environment in which they will thrive, pass on this truly exotic pet — but do find a petting zoo and actually meet a capybara. They should be on any animal lover's list of life experiences because there's simply no other creature quite like them.

Relevant Websites

The Capybara Page
www.rebsig.com/capybara/

San Diego Zoo Animals
www.animals.sandiegozoo.org/animals/capybara

Capybara as Pets - The Giant Rodent
www.capybarafacts.com/Capybara-as-Pets.html

CapybaraWorld
www.capybaraworld.wordpress.com/

Pets 101 - Capybara (Animal Planet)
www.youtube.com/watch?v=DYGz3xqiR2U

Wikipedia Information - Capybara
www.en.wikipedia.org/wiki/Capybara

ZooBorns: Capybara
www.zooborns.com/zooborns/capybara/

Animal Diversity Web
www.animaldiversity.ummz.umich.edu/accounts/Hydroch
oerus_hydrochaeris/

BBC Nature Wildlife - Capybara
www.bbc.co.uk/nature/life/Capybara

a-z animals
www.a-z-animals.com/animals/capybara/

Conservation International
www.legacy.earlham.edu/~martilu/capybarapage.htm

Animal Fact Guide
www.animalfactguide.com/animal-facts/capybara/

Caplin Rous
www.jeffvandermeer.com/2009/06/24/the-fantastical-capybara-an-interview-with-typaldos-about-caplin-rous/

Capybara Information
www.capybaras.net/

Dobbye The Capybara
www.petcapybara.com/

Caplin Rous and Garibaldi Rous
Capybara Madness
http://gianthamster.com/

Glossary

B

bedding - Any material used in an animal's habitat as substrate. With capybara, hay or grass and soil is typically used in outside enclosures.

C

cecum - The cecum is an enlarged portion of the capybara's digestive tract between the small and large intestine. Beneficial bacteria in the cecum aids in breaking down ingested plant material.

coprophagous - Animals that eat their own feces to aid in the maintenance of gut flora and the efficient digestion of high cellulose content in the diet are said to be coprophagnous.

crepuscular - Animals that are most active at dawn and dusk are said to be crepuscular.

G

gestation - The period of time that elapses between conception and birth.

H

herbivore - An animal whose primary source of nutrition is derived from plant material.

herd - The nomenclature for a large group of capybaras, especially in the wild.

M

malocclusion - A dental condition in which the teeth of a capybara overgrow preventing the animal from eating.

mange - A skin condition that presents with severe itching. Caused by a burrowing mite.

morillo - A bare, raised scent gland located on the nose of a capybara. It is present in both males and females, but is more prominent in males.

N

neutering - The surgical removal of a male capybara's testicles to prevent the animal from impregnating a female.

nocturnal - Animals that are most active at night and that sleep during the day are said to be nocturnal.

R

rodent - A gnawing mammal in the order Rodentia, which includes rats and mice, but also squirrels, hamsters, porcupines, and capybaras.

S

scurvy - A nutritional deficiency in capybaras that occurs when they do not receive adequate amounts of Vitamin C.

semi-aquatic - Any group of animals that live near and spend part of their time in the water.

spaying - The surgical removal of a female capybara's reproductive organs.

substrate - Another term for the material used to line the bottom of an animal's habitat. Also called bedding or litter.

Index

Lightning Source UK Ltd.
Milton Keynes UK
UKOW05f2345211216
290628UK00015B/237/P